Your Pet Dinosaur

An Owner's Manual
By Dr. Rex
of The Museum of Relatively Natural History

As Told to and Illustrated by
HUDSON TALBOTT

MORROW JUNIOR BOOKS
New York

Mixed media were used for the full-color artwork.
The text type is 15-point Caxton Roman Light.

Printed in the United States of America.
1 2 3 4 5 6 7 8 9 10

Library of Congress Cataloging-in-Publication Data
Talbott, Hudson.
    Your pet dinosaur / Hudson Talbott.
        p.   cm.
    Summary: Offers humorous advice on the care and feeding of
different kinds of dinosaurs as pets.
    ISBN 0-688-11337-0. — ISBN 0-688-11338-9 (lib. bdg.).
    1. Wit and humor, Juvenile.   2. Dinosaurs—Juvenile humor.
3. Pets—Juvenile humor.   I. Title.
PN6163.T35   1992
818'.5407—dc20   91-39762   CIP   AC

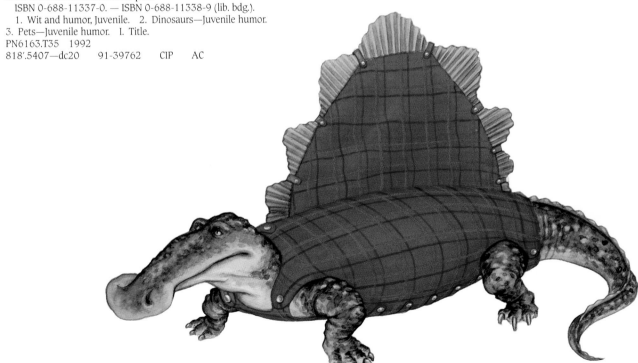

Contents

A Word from the Author

Hi, folks! It's me, Rex, under all these pups. We're back! Well, *I*'m back, and this time I want to get up close and personal because we need to talk dinos! Yes, you've read the books, you've seen the movies, and yet there's still something missing, a certain emptiness in your life. Perhaps you've finally admitted to yourself that *you* need a dino to call your very own. Well, I feel the same about you, but I can't leave my work, and besides, there are so many great dino pups just waiting to be adopted. You're looking to find out the who, what, where, when, why, and how of dinos, so let's take it from the top!

Why a Dino? Why Not a Hamster?

There's something about a dino that's unlike other pets. Is it our smile? The way we cha-cha? The way we can catch a Frisbee without drooling all over it? Perhaps *pet* isn't even the right word for us. I prefer to think of dinos as foreign-exchange students from another era. We have so much to learn from each other! And we don't smell like cedar chips.

Choosing the Right Dino

The "right" dino really depends on you. You need to ask yourself some important questions, such as:

- Do I want him to sit on my lap or do I want to sit on his?
- Do I *really* want a new family member or just to get rid of some of the old ones?
- Do I want a soul mate for life or am I just looking for someone to help me with long division?
- Would a meat-eater be as concerned about endangered species as a vegetarian?

And last, but not least:

- How much is it gonna cost me?

Your choice ultimately depends on your life-style and your needs. There are four basic types of dinos—the manglers, the shredders, the squashers, and the bone-crushers—and in each group there are dozens of breeds to choose from. One of them will be just right for you!

A budding little buckaroo takes a ride on his new megalasaurus, an excellent choice for a first mount, due to its docile nature and reluctance to chew the hand that feeds them.

Bringing the "Baby" Home

There's nothing quite as exciting as the day the new family member arrives. He/she will probably be a bit nervous and need to tear up a room or two before settling down and feeling at home. Remember, your new dino is still going through the trauma of being taken away from his mother, so give him the run of the house while it's still standing. The days of discipline come soon enough, and this is a way to show how much you love your pet.

The First Night

The true test of a dino owner comes on the first night, when the howling begins. The cry of a lonely dino evokes all the pain and agony the world has suffered since time began. "What's happened to my species?" he seems to wail. "Oh, fate, what cruel trick have you played on my people? We, who once ruled the earth, must now suffer alone in somebody's laundry room with only a hot-water bottle for company? What's to become of me? Oh, little two-legged creature who dragged me from my loved ones, you hold my fate in your hands! Have mercy, I beg you!"

So bring him a sandwich. Otherwise, you'll never hear the end of it.

When introducing a new pet to one who is used to having your place to himself, it's important not to rush things. Give the two of them the space they need to get acquainted in their own way. Dinos have a simple method of working out questions of seniority—just keep the mop and bandages handy.

Feeding

This comes rather naturally to the dino, so you won't have to worry much about technique. There is a marked difference, however, between the frisky little dino pup and her full-grown counterpart, illustrated below. The enthusiasm of a hungry pup is boundless! Therefore, a reinforced concrete feeding pen with a hole to throw food through is recommended to reduce risk of accidental loss of limbs. Breeders usually feed the little nippers separately to avoid "feeding frenzies," where the line between fellow pups and dinner often becomes blurred.

Mature dinos have a more discreet palate and often enjoy combining their own dietary needs with their concern for the environment.

NONALCOHOLIC, GRAPE-COLORED DIET BEVERAGE

REUSABLE BOTTLE

RECYCLABLE CORK

NONFAT, LOW-CHOLESTEROL CHEESE SUBSTITUTE

WOOD (A RENEWABLE RESOURCE)

Speaking of the environment, that takes us to our next topic.

Housebreaking

Housebreaking often lives up to its name, especially if we're talking about a pterosaur who's claimed the roof. Just think of it as lots and lots and lots of free fertilizer! It would also pay to invest in a heavy-duty pooper-scooper, or, in the case of the brontosaurus, a pooper steam shovel.

Discipline,
or "Wait 'Til Your Father Gets Home!"

Ninety-nine percent of the time, pups aren't aware that they've done something wrong. But ignorance of the law is no excuse. Try to catch them in the act and scold them immediately. "Shame on you!" is always a good standby. Or how about 酏兒 酏兒! (It's never too early to start them in foreign languages.)

Occasionally, incriminating evidence will turn up—a mailman's pouch, say, or the rhinestone collar of the neighbor's poodle. Show them to the "suspect" and gauge his reaction. A tucked-under tail means he's guilty of something. A wagging tail means, "They were delicious. Are there seconds?" This is probably his idea of a joke, but you may want to check with the neighbors and the post office just to make sure.

Fitting the punishment to the crime is important. It's one thing for a young pup to chew up a couch and quite another for him to be caught passing bad checks, trading stocks on Wall Street with insider information, or using your phone card to call the Dino Date Line. Remember—it's only a phase. Usually.

Young, teething triceratopses love to gnaw on everything! Don't tempt them by leaving your furniture around the house.

Setting Limits

Dinos are like kids. They need to know what their limits are—so they can step over them. As the new "parent," it's your job to give little Muffy the discipline structure she needs to feel safe and secure. Should a "no-no" occur, a little tap on the snout or hindquarters with a rolled-up newspaper will usually make little Spike see the error of his ways.

If you don't believe in spanking of any kind, you might try a new kitchen gizmo called the Whip 'n' Chill Blaster. Designed originally for mass-producing cafeteria desserts, it has proven effective in the home as a gentle "persuader." It allows you to conveniently send two messages at once: "You've stepped out-of-line, but, because I love you, here's your favorite dessert." It's a sweet way to provide the guidance they're seeking.

Ms. Rose Evans tries out a new Raspberry Fluff on naughty Bingo.

Like dogs and cats, dinos will try to establish their territory by marking it with their own scent. A good sturdy fence will reduce the number of border disputes, but if a disagreement should occur, a splash of water and a sharp reprimand ought to restore peace.

Exercise—the Basics

Keeping fit is just as important for your pet as it is for you, and getting started with an exercise program is probably a good idea for both of you.

Exercise can take a wide variety of forms. The one you choose should depend on the breed, age, and personality of your pet. And it needn't be boring. For example:

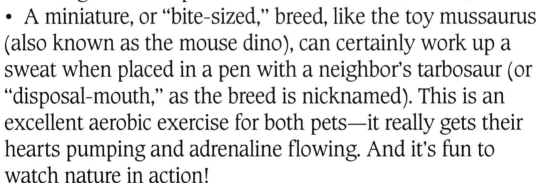

• A miniature, or "bite-sized," breed, like the toy mussaurus (also known as the mouse dino), can certainly work up a sweat when placed in a pen with a neighbor's tarbosaur (or "disposal-mouth," as the breed is nicknamed). This is an excellent aerobic exercise for both pets—it really gets their hearts pumping and adrenaline flowing. And it's fun to watch nature in action!

• Like their elephantine cousins, the woolly mammoths love the water, so the beach is the perfect place to combine work-out and play. What a great way to get closer to your pet! Just be careful of those swinging tusks.

Mammoths will play "catch" in the surf for hours. You may want to run them through a car wash afterward, to rinse out the salt.

17

Exercise—from Dino to Dynamo

For the saddle-bred dinos, especially the two-seaters and four-seaters, schooling begins with a workout on the lead, or "lunge line." Care should be taken to follow accurately the method shown, or the benefit of exercise will be diminished.

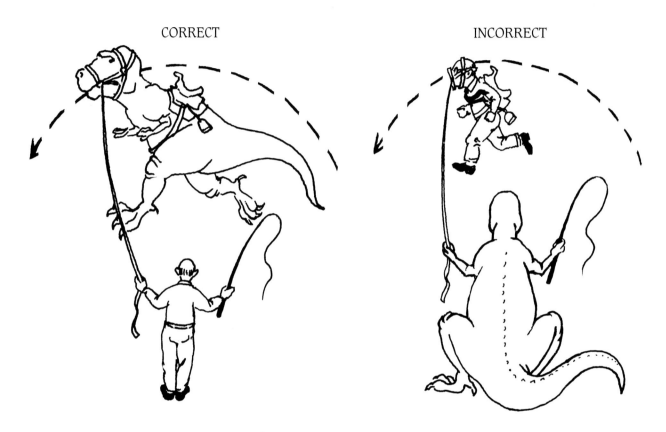

CORRECT   INCORRECT

A group exercise that's quickly becoming a neighborhood favorite is the "bronto stampede." All it takes is a dozen or so of those ten-ton "nervous Nellies" and one hungry-looking carnivore to get the fun started. You *and* your pet can enjoy all the action as long as you can stay *ahead* of the thundering herd. You may want to let little Fifi or Boris off the leash for this one.

And don't forget every owner's favorite exercise—"Fetch!"

Obedience Training

Dinos are eager to please. Almost all of them enjoy responding to commands, because they know what it does for their owner's ego. The owner feels important, the dino gets fed, and they both feel loved. Intelligence, body weight, and size all play a part in how different breeds will respond. For example, it's a major victory to get a brachiosaurus just to sit, while tyrannosaurs will take any command and put their own "spin" on it. Cousin Willy demonstrates some old standards:

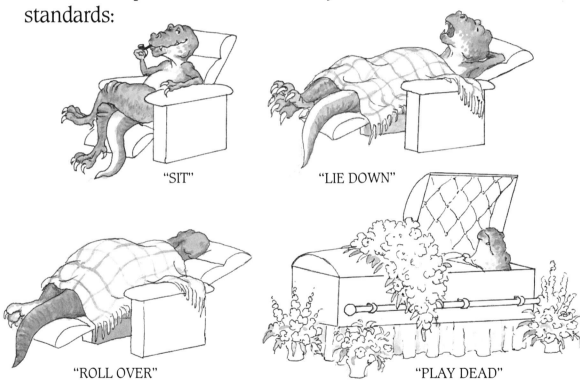

"SIT"

"LIE DOWN"

"ROLL OVER"

"PLAY DEAD"

Rewards and Treats

Discipline, obedience, exercise—your pet has been working hard to please you. Isn't it time you thanked him or her in a special way? A new toy, perhaps, or a new hat, or even a little pet to call his very own (for vegetarian dinos only).

Outings can be real treats for dinos, and letting them choose the event is a great way of saying, "Thank you, for just being you!"

Dino Body Language

Dinos are remarkably clever when it comes to communicating. Most signals sent by body language are easy to read because they're familiar to us. A smile says, "I'm happy." A wagging tail means, "I'm very happy," or, in the case of the stegosaurus with the two-foot-long spikes on his tail, "I'm sorry I'm destroying your house by wagging my tail, but I can't help it 'cause I'm so happy."

Listed below are a few of the less-easy-to-read gestures. On occasion, they actually mean something, but usually they're just done out of boredom.

KNOCKING: A banging of the head on top of the television set indicates a wish to change the channel.

JITTERFEET: Nervous dancing—often seen in brontosauruses when carnivores are visiting. Can cause damage to furniture and floors.

SNORING: A loud nasal drone, usually heard from tyrannosaurs when relatives are visiting. Can cause damage to ceiling plaster and family relationships.

CHOKING: Pet places claws around his/her own neck, turns purple, and keels over. A standard attempt to gain attention; often applied to pet owner's neck if first attempt fails.

DROOLING: Profuse salivation accompanied by a blank stare; he's either pretending he's the vice president or he has rabies.

DANCE OF ECSTASY (shown above): Performed on back, with limbs twitching and flailing in all directions. Usually due to tummy being scratched, but can also result from a bag of double-fudge brownies. Often accompanied by gurgles, squeaks, purring, and howls of glee. Caution: Always stand clear of the hind legs.

Quirks and How to Deal with Them

Each dino is different and needs to be treated that way. Certain breeds and certain individuals have their own little quirks. Here are some tips to remember.

1. Never draw attention to a hadrosaur's physical appearance.

2. The deinonychus loves a party, but his slow wit and quick jaws can lead to social embarrassment. Make sure he's fed before guests arrive, and avoid confusing him with phrases like "We're having Spike and Muffy for dinner tonight."

3. A pregnant tarbosaur will often build false "nests" in odd locations. BMW convertibles are a favorite choice because their soft leather upholstery is easily shredded to make comfy bedding. You may wish to alert the neighbors.

4. The "split personality" is often a problem for the archaeopteryx, or bird dino. Be patient while they flutter and/or stomp their way through the crisis, and keep feeding them their favorite treat—steak 'n' birdseed. If the problem persists, you may wish to seek professional help. This is covered in the next section.

When Good Dinos Go Bad

Bad dinos are not born—they're made. Sometimes this "acting out" is a way of saying, "You don't understand me," or "You always loved Muffy more than me," or "I didn't mean to eat him; it just happened."

We all have a need to express ourselves. In fact, more often than not, the pet owner is the one with the problem and the pet is simply trying to express it for him. Make sure you're sending the right signals the next time little Bubba terrorizes the neighborhood, devours a couch, steps on a baby-sitter, or eats peanut butter right out of the jar. Haven't we *all* wanted to do these things at some point? Understanding and patience go a long way here. *Remember—he's only trying to win your love!*

There are occasions when seeking "professional help" is in order. A good example of this is the "split personality" in the archaeopteryx, or bird dino. Left untreated, a pet can turn quite vicious (Figure A). But a few months of therapy can give your pet a whole new outlook (Figure B).

A.

Love your hairdo, dear—even more now than when it was in style

B.

.... and that hairdo grows more becoming with each passing decade

The heartbreak of delinquent dinos.

Adolescent dinos can show a drastic change in behavior. For most, it's just a passing phase, but there are those who answer the call of the wild with a roar of an engine and a howl from the soul. Most often, therapy helps bring these explosive emotions under control. If it doesn't—run.

Young Dinos in Love

Your pet has finally come to the stage when there's something on his or her mind other than dinner. It would be nice if we could spare little Spike the pain of a broken heart, but you would have better luck reasoning with an oncoming diesel than a lovesick dino. Just try to understand what he's going through, and bear in mind that falling in love is one of life's major "growth experiences." (Try to remember this when you get the phone bill.)

Ask Dr. Rex

Q. Are you really a doctor?

A. I'm glad you asked that, for it's important that you know who the experts *really* are! You don't want to place your trust in just anyone. It's a question that needs to be asked over and over again.

Q. But are you a doctor?

A. You're absolutely right to inquire about this and I've always believed in being totally open and honest about it. Honesty is always the best policy. It's as simple as that.

Q. Will you answer my question?

A. Do I detect some hostility here? Why the anger? Perhaps you need to consult another sort of doctor about your problem. Besides, I didn't hear the magic words.

Q. Will you *please* answer the question? *Thank you.*

A. Well, I'll repeat what I've already said—my position on this is perfectly clear; it's on the record, and I stand by it.

Q. Are you planning to run for public office?

A. I don't know what gave you that idea, but thanks for asking and thanks for your support. Next question.

Q. Should I take my pet on vacation?

A. That depends on where you're going—Aunt Irma's in Detroit or the French Riviera.

Q. Aunt Irma's.

A. In that case, be sure the fridge is well stocked, the Pizza Hut's number is by the phone, and the VCR is working before pulling out of the drive and waving good-bye to little Spike and Muffy. And say hi to Aunt Irma for us.

Q. What are the most common names for dinosaurs?

A. Spike and Muffy.

Q. Is it true that pets and their owners begin to look alike?

A. Oh, please! Let's move on to the next topic.

Show Dinos

Here are last year's grand-prize winners of the National Dino Show held at Fossil Bluffs, Idaho. Anyone can look at these beauties and see that this is what "pure-bred" is all about!

FIRST PRIZE—BEST IN SHOW

Ms. Ludmila Grunchcov and "Gorbi"
Brighton Beach, New York

SECOND PRIZE
Dr. Seymour Fleegle
and "Mr. Burp"
Oatmeal Plains, Ohio

THIRD PRIZE
Mr. Lester Nurdlinger
and "Chrome-Dome"
Kankakee, Illinois

THE JUDGES PANEL

Dear Dr. Rex

Dear Dr. Rex,

I don't know what's come over my stegosaur, Ralph, lately. Whenever I begin practicing my trombone, he insists on dragging me up the basement stairs, tossing me on the front lawn, and giving me mouth-to-mouth resuscitation. What's going on here?

Signed,
Steg-gravated
Staten Island, N.Y.

Dear Steg,

Ralph's not lost his little pea-sized mind, he's just trying to save your life. Back in the old days (I'm talking Early Triassic), we all used little danger signals to warn one another. My guess is that when Ralph hears your trombone-playing, he thinks the house is on fire. Just plug up Ralph's earholes the next time you want to practice, and reward him with a little fireman's hat of his own. He'll be as happy as a clam (and not much brighter).

Dear Dr. Rex,

Reggie, our three-year-old megalasaur, is a real "people dino," but this enthusiasm can be a problem. Every time he sees someone new, he has to leap on them. We were in the emergency room four times last week, and our mailman will be in traction for at least six months. My insurance won't cover much more of this. What to do?

Signed,
Licking Our Wounds
Pez, Indiana

Dear Licking,

Reggie needs to share his feelings for others. Any interference at this stage could cause permanent damage to his emotional growth. And since most of your friends are already protected by body casts, why not let him express himself? Besides, the world could use a little more love.

Dear Dr. Rex,

We took in a stray tyrannosaur a while back. He must have been near starvation because he went through the fridge, the freezer, and the cupboards like a vacuum cleaner. The kids loved him, but my husband got tired of finding him asleep in the Barcalounger clutching the T.V. remote control. The poor creature vanished one night. Do you think he starved to death?

Signed,
Guilt-ridden in Omaha

Dear G.R.,

Was that *you* in Nebraska? Sorry I left so abruptly, but Julia Child invited me to dinner in Boston, and I managed to get on a late flight. I guess I forgot to write a thank-you note, but I'll never forget *you*. Or your corn dogs. And we'll always have Omaha!

The Well-Dressed Dino

I've often looked at my species and thought, When you have as much style as we do, who needs clothes? Yet smart dinos everywhere understand the importance of dressing right. Youngsters love to show how trendy they are, while older, more conservative dinos know nothing radiates success more than a "power plaid."

Fashion Don'ts for Dinos

You can help your pet create a tasteful "look" by bringing out your dino's natural elegance. Fashion trends may come and go, but *Style* is never out of style. In any case, try to avoid:

Spike Heels
Bad for posture and you'll never find their size.

Horn Warmers
Makes them look nerdy. Triceratops need no help in this department.

Polka Dots
Tarbosaurs get rather testy about busy prints. Paisleys are a problem, too.

Turtlenecks

The back spikes on an ankylosaur are a problem. Once on, it does nothing to hide the "ank's" tendency toward pudginess.

Letting Dinos Dress Themselves

Left to their own devices, it's usually one sad misstep from fashion statement to overstatement for the dino with an overindulgent "parent."

Working Dinos

Besides all the joy that dinos bring as pets, there are many around the world who enjoy brilliant "careers." Here are two examples:

Romanian Sheep Dinos:
It's always a pleasure to watch a precision team of "Romies" in action. You can still see them hard at work in the tranquil solitude of their native Carpathian mountains.

Pteranodon Retrievers
"Pteris" are born bargain hunters. A sale gives them a
chance to spread their wings and express their natural flair
for lingerie.

What pride and satisfaction you'll both feel as he fox-trots you 'round the club dance floor—off the leash!

You and Your Dino—the Golden Years

Nothing compares to the pleasure that you and your scaly friend will share as you enter "the golden years" of your relationship. All the time and energy that you poured into raising and training your dino will finally make sense as the light of companionship comes shining through.

Scientific research has proven that owning a pet can reduce stress and promote a sense of contentment and well-being. Just ask most owners and they'll agree: Despite their own hectic, anxiety-ridden lives, their pets have apparently found complete inner peace.

But most dinos would be the first to insist that they owe their happiness to your loving support. And isn't that feeling mutual? If there's someone loving you without regard to your looks, money, achievements, status—or even species— what else matters? At the end of the day, when all is said and done…

...it's nice to come home to a hug.